# Southern Winds
## jazz flute jam

C - B♭ - E♭ INSTRUMENTS

MUSIC MINUS ONE

3376

## SUGGESTIONS FOR USING THIS MMO EDITION

**W**E HAVE TRIED to create a product that will provide you an easy way to learn and perform these compositions with a full ensemble in the comfort of your own home.

We have observed generally accepted tempi, and always in the originally intended key, but some may wish to perform at a different tempo, or to slow down or speed up the accompaniment for practice purposes; or to alter the piece to a more comfortable key. For maximum flexibility, you can purchase from MMO specialized CD players & recorders which allow variable speed while maintaining proper pitch, and vice versa. This is an indispensable tool for the serious musician and you may wish to look into purchasing this useful piece of equipment for full enjoyment of all your MMO editions.

We want to provide you with the most useful practice and performance accompaniments possible. If you have any suggestions for improving the MMO system, please feel free to contact us. You can reach us by e-mail at *info@musicminusone.com*.

3376

# CONTENTS

ISBN 1-59615-673-2

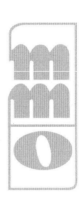

# C instrument parts

C INSTRUMENTS

# Blue Bossa

Music by Kenny Dorham

AFTER SOLOS, D.S. AL CODA

C Instruments

# Feel Like Makin' Love

Music by Eugene McDaniels

REPEAT TO A FOR SOLOS THEN D.S. AL CODA

MMO 3376

# Little Linda

Music by Jeremy Wall

MMO3376

# Comin' Home Baby

Music by Earl Hagan

Repeat to A for solos, then D.S. al coda

# BLACK ORPHEUS

C INSTRUMENTS

# MEDITATION

MUSIC BY ANTONIO CARLOS JOBIM
LYRIC BY NORMAN GIMBEL

REPEAT TO A FOR SOLOS, THEN D.S. AL CODA

MMO 3376

# Samba de Orfeo

Music by Antonio Maria and Luiz Bonfa

REPEAT TO A FOR SOLOS, THEN D.S. AL CODA

C Instruments

# Just Friends

Music by John Klenner
Lyric by Sam M. Lewis

C Instruments

# Mercy, Mercy, Mercy

Music by Josef Zawinul

18

# B♭ instrument parts

**Bb Instruments**

# Blue Bossa

Music by Kenny Dorham

After solos, D.S. al Coda

# Feel Like Makin' Love

**Bb INSTRUMENTS**

# LITTLE LINDA

Music by Jeremy Wall

**Bb INSTRUMENTS**

# COMIN' HOME BABY

Music by Earl Hagan

REPEAT TO A FOR SOLOS, THEN D.S. AL CODA

**Bb Instruments**

# Black Orpheus

Music by Luiz Bonfa

MMO3376

**Bb Instruments**

# Meditation

Music by Antonio Carlos Jobim
Lyric by Norman Gimbel

**Bb Instruments**

# Samba de Orfeo

Music by Antonio Maria and Luiz Bonfa

**Bb Instruments**

# Just Friends

Music by John Klenner
Lyric by Sam M. Lewis

REPEAT TO A FOR SOLOS

RIT.

**Bb Instruments**

# MERCY, MERCY, MERCY

Music by Josef Zawinul

# E♭ instrument parts

Eb INSTRUMENTS

# Blue Bossa

Music by Kenny Dorham

After solos, D.S. al Coda

Eb Instruments

# Feel Like Makin' Love

Music by Eugene McDaniels

Repeat to A for solos then D.S. al coda

# Little Linda

Music by Jeremy Wall

Eb INSTRUMENTS

# COMIN' HOME BABY

MUSIC BY EARL HAGAN

REPEAT TO A FOR SOLOS, THEN D.S. AL CODA

Eb Instruments

# Black Orpheus

Music by Luiz Bonfa

MMO3376

# MEDITATION

Music by Antonio Carlos Jobim
Lyric by Norman Gimbel

REPEAT TO A FOR SOLOS, THEN D.S. AL CODA

Eb INSTRUMENTS

# SAMBA DE ORFEO

MUSIC BY ANTONIO MARIA AND LUIZ BONFA

REPEAT TO A FOR SOLOS, THEN D.S. AL CODA

**Eb Instruments**

# JUST FRIENDS

Music by John Klenner
Lyric by Sam M. Lewis

REPEAT TO A FOR SOLOS

RIT.

**Eb Instruments**

# MERCY, MERCY, MERCY

Music by Josef Zawinul

RIT. LAST X

## MUSIC MINUS ONE

50 Executive Boulevard
Elmsford, New York 10523-1325
1.800.669.7464 (U.S.)/914.592.1188 (International)

www.musicminusone.com
e-mail: mmogroup@musicminusone.com